O'REILLY®
Strata
Making Data Work

Learn ho
data into decisions.

T0220864

From startups to the Fortune 500, smart companies are betting on data-driven insight, seizing the opportunities that are emerging from the convergence of four powerful trends:

- New methods of collecting, managing, and analyzing data

- Cloud computing that offers inexpensive storage and flexible, on-demand computing power for massive data sets

- Visualization techniques that turn complex data into images that tell a compelling story

- Tools that make the power of data available to anyone

Get control over big data and turn it into insight with O'Reilly's Strata offerings. Find the inspiration and information to create new products or revive existing ones, understand customer behavior, and get the data edge.

O'REILLY®

Visit oreilly.com/data to learn more.

Getting Started with GEO, CouchDB, and Node.js

Getting Started with GEO, CouchDB, and Node.js

Mick Thompson

O'REILLY®

Beijing · Cambridge · Farnham · Köln · Sebastopol · Tokyo

Getting Started with GEO, CouchDB, and Node.js
by Mick Thompson

Published by O'Reilly Media, Inc., 1005 Gravenstein Highway North, Sebastopol, CA 95472.

O'Reilly books may be purchased for educational, business, or sales promotional use. Online editions are also available for most titles (*http://my.safaribooksonline.com*). For more information, contact our corporate/institutional sales department: (800) 998-9938 or *corporate@oreilly.com*.

Editors: Mike Hendrickson and Julie Steele	**Cover Designer:** Karen Montgomery
Production Editor: Kristen Borg	**Interior Designer:** David Futato
Proofreader: O'Reilly Production Services	**Illustrator:** Robert Romano

Printing History:

July 2011:	First Edition.

ISBN: 978-1-449-30752-3

[LSI]

1311082866

Table of Contents

Preface

Where. Whether it refers to where you have been, where you are, or where you are going, the concept of *where* is important. Where links data to the physical world. A shopping list can be a very useful collection of data on its own, but that data can be even more useful with more context. If you map the location of the stores needed for each item on the shopping list, then you can create an efficient route to acquire the items on the list. Driving directions, traffic information, and weather can impact the route. All of this data can be fetched based on the location data added to the simple shopping list.

Location can add a new filter or layer of insight into existing data. It makes all kinds of new applications possible. In the past, using location or geographic data meant using complex or at times expensive software. Datasets could be costly or hard to find. Developing using open source tools such as Node.js and CouchDB has recently made working with location data simple and fast.

Conventions Used in This Book

The following typographical conventions are used in this book:

Italic
: Indicates new terms, URLs, email addresses, filenames, and file extensions.

`Constant width`
: Used for program listings, as well as within paragraphs to refer to program elements such as variable or function names, databases, data types, environment variables, statements, and keywords.

`Constant width bold`
: Shows commands or other text that should be typed literally by the user.

`Constant width italic`
: Shows text that should be replaced with user-supplied values or by values determined by context.

This icon signifies a tip, suggestion, or general note.

 This icon indicates a warning or caution.

Using Code Examples

This book is here to help you get your job done. In general, you may use the code in this book in your programs and documentation. You do not need to contact us for permission unless you're reproducing a significant portion of the code. For example, writing a program that uses several chunks of code from this book does not require permission. Selling or distributing a CD-ROM of examples from O'Reilly books does require permission. Answering a question by citing this book and quoting example code does not require permission. Incorporating a significant amount of example code from this book into your product's documentation does require permission.

We appreciate, but do not require, attribution. An attribution usually includes the title, author, publisher, and ISBN. For example: "*Getting Started with GEO, CouchDB, and Node.js* by Mick Thompson (O'Reilly). Copyright 2011 David Thompson, 978-1-449-30752-3."

If you feel your use of code examples falls outside fair use or the permission given above, feel free to contact us at *permissions@oreilly.com*.

Safari® Books Online

Safari Safari Books Online is an on-demand digital library that lets you easily search over 7,500 technology and creative reference books and videos to find the answers you need quickly.

With a subscription, you can read any page and watch any video from our library online. Read books on your cell phone and mobile devices. Access new titles before they are available for print, and get exclusive access to manuscripts in development and post feedback for the authors. Copy and paste code samples, organize your favorites, download chapters, bookmark key sections, create notes, print out pages, and benefit from tons of other time-saving features.

O'Reilly Media has uploaded this book to the Safari Books Online service. To have full digital access to this book and others on similar topics from O'Reilly and other publishers, sign up for free at *http://my.safaribooksonline.com*.

How to Contact Us

Please address comments and questions concerning this book to the publisher:

O'Reilly Media, Inc.
1005 Gravenstein Highway North
Sebastopol, CA 95472
800-998-9938 (in the United States or Canada)
707-829-0515 (international or local)
707-829-0104 (fax)

We have a web page for this book, where we list errata, examples, and any additional information. You can access this page at:

http://oreilly.com/catalog/97814493075232

To comment or ask technical questions about this book, send email to:

bookquestions@oreilly.com

For more information about our books, courses, conferences, and news, see our website at *http://www.oreilly.com*.

Find us on Facebook: *http://facebook.com/oreilly*

Follow us on Twitter: *http://twitter.com/oreillymedia*

Watch us on YouTube: *http://www.youtube.com/oreillymedia*

CHAPTER 1

Node.js

Node.js has quickly become a very popular asynchronous framework for JavaScript. It is built on top of the same V8 engine that the Chromium and Google Chrome web browsers use to interpret JavaScript. With the addition of networking and file system API support, it has quickly proved to be a capable tool for interacting with IO in a asynchronous way.

There are many other libraries in several other languages that can accomplish the same asynchronous handling of IO. There are different conventions, schools of thought, and preferences of developers. Node.js uses callbacks for the developer to notified of the progress of asynchronous operations. Callbacks are nothing new for developers accustom to Python's Twisted library or other similar frameworks. Callbacks can be a very easy and powerful way to manage the flow of an appilication, but as with anything new they also offer an opportunity to trip up a developer. The first thing to keep in mind when getting started with asynchronous development is that execution might not follow the same squence every time.

Getting Started with Node.js

In order to install Node.js, download the source and build it. The main Node.js web page at *http://nodejs.org* can be very helpful in linking to downloads, source code repositories, and documentation. The master branch of the repository is kept in a semi-unstable state, so before building check out the most recent tagged version. For example: v0.4.9.

The Node.js package manager or NPM is an extremely useful tool. It can handle installing, updating, and removing packages and their dependencies. Creating packages is also simple since the configuration for the package is contained in the package.json file. Installation instructions for NPM are included in the Node.js repository.

Asynchronous Callbacks

An Example case to show how asynchronous IO works is to make two HTTP requests and then combine the results. In the first example the request to the second web API will be nested in the callback from the first. This might seem like the easiest way to combine the results, but will not be the most effective usage of asynchronous IO.

Google provides an API that returns the elevation for a given latitude and longitude. The example requests will be of two points random points on Earth. To start create a function that will handles the request to the Google elevation API as well as parses the response:

```
var http = require("http"),
    sys = require("sys");

function getElevation(lat,lng, callback){
    var options = {
        host: 'maps.googleapis.com',
        port: 80,
        path: '/maps/api/elevation/json?locations='+lat+','+lng+'&sensor=true'
    };
    http.get(options, function(res) {
        data = "";
        res.on('data', function (chunk) {
                data += chunk;
            });
        res.on('end', function (chunk) {
                el_response = JSON.parse(data);
                callback(el_response.results[0].elevation);
            });
    });
}
```

In order to run the requests sequentially, the call to fetch the second elevation is in the callback for the first:

```
var elevations= []
getElevation(40.714728,-73.998672, function(elevation){
        elevations.push(elevation);
        getElevation(-40.714728,73.998672, function(elevation){
                elevations.push(elevation);
                console.log("Elevations: "+elevations);
            });
});
```

This will add the two elevations in order to the elevations array. However, the program will wait for the first request to finish before making the second request. The amount of time fetching the two elevations can be reduced by making the initial requests in parallel and combining the results in the callback:

```
var elevations= [];
function elevationResponse(elevation){
    elevations.push(elevation);
```

```
    if(elevations.length == 2){
        console.log("Elevations: "+elevations);
    }
}

getElevation(40.714728,-73.998672, elevationResponse);
getElevation(-40.714728, 73.998672, elevationResponse);
```

Now the callback checks to see if the combined data is complete; in this case, it checks to see if there are two items in the array.

Sometimes the first response callback gets called before the second, and sometimes it does not. Since the requests are carried out at the same time and they can take a variable ammount of time, it isnt guaranteed what order the callback functions will be called in. But what if this data needs to be displayed in order?

There are cases that require nesting the call to another function in a callback—perhaps if the response to the first request was going to provide the needed data to make the second request. In that case, there is no choice but to wait, and make the second request after the first.

In the elevation example, there is no need to wait. Both requests can be made at the same timea and the results can be combined later. By adding a function to correctly combine the data and using that as the response callback, the data can then be presented in the correct order every time.

By doing these two requests asynchronously, the execution time is reduced. This makes the app more responsive to the user, and frees the app to do other needed processing while waiting on IO tasks. A quick timing of the two methods show the difference in time needed to fetch the same data.

```
hostname $ time node elevation_request.js

Elevations: 8.883694648742676,-3742.2880859375

real    0m0.627s
user    0m0.076s
sys     0m0.029s

hostname $ time node elevation_request2.js
Elevations: 8.883694648742676,-3742.2880859375

real    0m0.340s
user    0m0.074s
sys     0m0.027s
```

In other languages this can be accomplished through threading, in many cases. Threads are sometimes messy to work with, as they require synchronizing or locking in order to manipulate shared memory safely. The forced Asnychronous IO of Node.js gives a clean way to accomplish parallel tasks.

Using Node.js on the Web

One of the many uses of Node.js is to serve up dynamic content over HTTP: that is to say, websites. Again another advanage of Node.js's Asynchronous IO is the preformance of handling many requests at same time. There is a maturing list of modules and frameworks to handle some of the common tasks of a web server. ConnectJS is an HTTP server module that has a collection of plugins that provide logging, cookie parsing, session management and much more.

ExpressJS

Built on top of ConnectJS is ExpressJS framework. ExpressJS extends ConnectJS adding robust routing, view rendering, and templating. Using ExpressJS, it is easy to get a simple web server up and running. ExpressJS can be installed using npm:

```
hostname $ npm install express
```

Routes

There are only a few lines of code needed to start a server and handle a URL route:

```
var express = require('express');
var app = express.createServer();

app.get('/', function(req, res){
    res.send('nodejs!');
});

app.listen(3000);
```

Run this with Node.js:

```
hostname $ node app.js
```

This server can now be reached at *http://localhost:3000/*.

When setting up a route in ExpressJS, the second argument is a callback function. The callback is executed when the route matches the requested URL. The callback is passed two arguments. First, a request object that contains all the information about that HTTP request. Second a response object which has member functions that manipulate the HTTP response.

The param function on the request object parses parameters that are in the query string or in the post body. The function returns the value or an optional default value that is set using the second argument to the function:

```
app.get('/echo', function(req, res){
    echo = req.param("echo", "no param")
    res.send('ECHO: '+echo);
});
```

Templates

The response object has member functions which can be used to set the headers and the status code, return files, or simply return a text response body as above. The response object also handles rendering templates:

```
app.get('/template', function(req, res){
    res.render('index.ejs', { title: 'New Template Page', layout: true });
});
```

The above code will looks for the template named index.ejs by default in a directory named views and replaces the template variables with the set passed into the render function:

```
<h1><%= title %></h1>
```

ExpressJS supports several templating markups, and of course can be extended to support others. These include the following:

- Haml: A haml implementation
- Jade: The haml.js successor
- EJS: Embedded JavaScript
- CoffeeKup: CoffeeScript based templating
- jQuery: Templates for node

Static Files

ExpressJS can also serve up static files such as images, client side JavaScript, and style-sheets. The first argument to the use function specifies a base route. The second argument specifics the local directory to serve static files from. In this case, files in the static directory will be accessible along the same path:

```
app.use('/static', express.static(__dirname + '/static'));
// This mean the file "static/client.js" will be available at
// http://localhost:3000/static/client.js
```

ExpressJS handles many other aspects of running a HTTP server, including session support, routing middleware, cookie parsing, and many other things. The full documentation for ExpressJS is provided at *http://expressjs.com/guide.html*

Node.js with its powerful asynchronous IO, common and simple syntax, and many useful modules in active development is a great choice for building web applications.

CHAPTER 2

Geographic Data

Geographic data comes in many formats. So many in fact, there could easily be a book based just on that subject, but to keep this simpler, here is an explanation of a few of the most common ones.

Shapefiles are one of the most common formats. The format was created and is maintained by ESRI, who also sells many tools for manipulating data in that format. The also sell other popular closed source GIS server and client software. The format is a mostly open specification for GIS data. Shapefiles spatially describe geometries, those can include points, polygons, and lines. A shapefile comes as a collection of files. At least 3 are required: .shp, .shx, and .dbf. Those files define shapes (the geometry), an index of the geometry features, and attributes for those features, respectively.

Shapefiles are widely available. Many government agencies use this format to publish public data. In fact, much of the data from free sources, public government data, or even data published by corporations will often times be in shapefiles. Learning to convert those shapefiles for usage in other formats is very useful.

Geo Datasets

There are many places that host public domained geographic data. Here is a small collection:

US Census (http://www.census.gov/geo/www/tiger/tgrshp2010/tgrshp2010.html)
    The data is provided as shapefiles per state. This data is very complete and updated every 10 years. The last update was in 2010.

Natural Earth Data (http://www.naturalearthdata.com/)
    This is a collection of free and open datasets ranging from country level shapefiles of the world to many natural features including water, mountains, and geographic regions.

Global Administrative Areas (http://gadm.org/)
>A very complete set of administrative areas world wide. This includes country, state or province, county in some cases, and cities.

Consortium for Spatial Information (http://www.cgiar-csi.org)
>Datasets here include climate, elevation, soil, poverty. As well as links to other great sources for worldwide data.

Food and Agriculture Organization of the United Nations (http://www.fao.org/geonet work)
>This data goes well beyond the common administrative boundaries available and includes wildlife, land usage, forestry, human heath, and infrastructure among other things.

GeoJSON

GeoJSON is a standard for encoding spatial data using JSON (JavsScript Object No-tation). Since JSON has become the main data format for APIs on the web, it makes sense to standardize the way we represent geospatial data. GeoJSON is very easy to figure out, straightforward to parse, and simple to output. It supports many Geometry types.

Example Geometries

Here is a point in GeoJSON (the coordinates are ordered longitude, latitude):

```
{ "type": "Point", "coordinates": [100.0, 0.0] }
```

Here is a polygon in GeoJSON. Holes can be added in the polygon by adding more elements to the coordinates array:

```
{ "type": "Polygon",
  "coordinates": [
    [ [100.0, 0.0], [101.0, 0.0], [101.0, 1.0], [100.0, 1.0], [100.0, 0.0] ]
    ]
}
```

GeoJSON also defines Features and Feature Collections. With features you can asso-ciate identifiers, and properties with your geometry or Geometry Collection:

```
{ "type": "Feature",
  "geometry": {
    "type": "LineString",
    "coordinates": [
      [102.0, 0.0], [103.0, 1.0], [104.0, 0.0], [105.0, 1.0]
      ]
  },
  "properties": {
    "prop0": "value0",
    "prop1": 0.0
```

```
    }
}
```

 CouchDB which will be discussed further in this book stores JSON encoded documents. So, for all of the geospatial functionality found in CouchDB the data will need to be in the GeoJSON format.

GDAL

GDAL (Geospatial Data Abstraction Library) is arguably the most useful geospatial library in existence. It is included as a dependency of many other geospatial libraries that deal with reading or writing geospatial data in any of the common formats. There are bindings for GDAL in many languages which make it even more useful. GDAL is used for raster geodata, but the subproject OGR (Simple Feature Library) provides read/write access for a wide variety of vector geospatial formats. This includes ESRI shapefiles, KML, and some database formats.

Ogr includes several helpful command-line utilities. Those will be discussed after we install GDAL.

Installing

Most systems have GDAL packages available, like apt-get or yum (or on OSX, homebrew) that should be able to install it as well as all of its dependencies:

```
hostname $ brew install gdal
```

Grab Some Data

Next, get some test data. The data conversion example project is available to clone on github.

 Not everyone is familiar with git. Git has become a widely used distributed version control system. Github has a great introductory help page at *http://help.github.com/*.

Also, all of the projects in the book can be found at *http://github.com/ dthompson*. Github also offers packaged download files as a means of getting the source code instead of using git.

```
hostname $ git clone https://github.com/dthompson/example_shapefile_to_geojson.git
Cloning into example_shapefile_to_geojson...
....
Unpacking objects: 100% (8/8), done.
```

This repository contains a directory named 110m_lakes that includes the shapefile data (taken from Natural Earth Data, *http://www.naturalearthdata.com/downloads/110m -physical-vectors/110mlakes-reservoirs/*). The first step is to see what is included in the shapefile.

Ogrinfo

There is an Ogr tool to explore vector geospatial file, ogrinfo. Ogrinfo shows both top level metadata for the vector data source as well as specfic layer information for data sources that contain multiple layers.

 Most of the tools that ogr provides allow for querying data by properties or bounds. This can be helpful in limiting the data being converted to only the certain region that is needed. More details on the options available can be found by running the commands with -h or browsing the online documentation: *http://www.gdal.org/ogr_utilities.html*.

```
hostname $ ogrinfo 110m_lakes/110m_lakes.shp
INFO: Open of `110m_lakes/110m_lakes.shp'
      using driver `ESRI Shapefile' successful.
1: 110m_lakes (Polygon)
```

Ogr is using the ESRI shapefile driver. There is no real new information there, since that is the type of file used as input. The other information can be helpful. The shapefile only has 1 layer, named is 110m_lakes, containing polygon data. The layer's name can be used to find out more specifics about that layer. The option -so is used to output addition layer information and the name of the layer is passed as the second argument:

```
hostname $ ogrinfo -so 110m_lakes/110m_lakes.shp 110m_lakes
NFO: Open of `110m_lakes/110m_lakes.shp'
      using driver `ESRI Shapefile' successful.

Layer name: 110m_lakes
Geometry: Polygon
Feature Count: 26
Extent: (-124.953634, -16.536406) - (109.929807, 66.969298)
Layer SRS WKT:
GEOGCS["GCS_WGS_1984",
    DATUM["WGS_1984",
        SPHEROID["WGS_1984",6378137.0,298.257223563]],
    PRIMEM["Greenwich",0.0],
    UNIT["Degree",0.0174532925199433]]
ScaleRank: Integer (10.0)
FeatureCla: String (32.0)
Name1: String (254.0)
Name2: String (254.0)
```

Now there is a lot more information. The ouput contains the number of features in the layer, the extent that contains all the features, spatial reference system, and a list of attributes for each feature. There are four attributes: ScaleRank, FeatureCla (shorted from FeatureClass), Name1, and Name2. Each attribute also has detailed field info that includes the type as well as the max length of data in that field. This can all be useful to examine what data is in a shapefile before converting or importing it.

Ogr2ogr

The ogr2ogr command line tool handles reading, converting, and writing in the formats that ogr supports. This can used to easily convert the shapefile data to GeoJSON.

```
hostname $  ogr2ogr -f "GeoJSON" 110_lakes.json 110m_lakes/110m_lakes.shp
```

In this command, the format is specified by -f "GeoJSON". To see a list of available formats, use ogr2ogr --help. The next argument is the destination file, followed by the source file.

The output is a valid GeoJSON-encoded list of all the features from that shapefile, complete with attributes, saved to the destination file. Here is a small sample of the output:

```
{
  "type": "Feature",
  "properties": {
    "ScaleRank": 0,
    "FeatureCla": "Lake",
    "Name1": "Lake\rMichigan",
    "Name2": ""
  },
  "geometry": {
    "type": "Polygon",
    "coordinates": [
      [ [-85.539993,46.030007], ...]
    ]
  }
}
```

Geohash

Geohash is an algorithm that was created by Gustavo Niemeyer in 2008. By interleaving latitude and longitude in a bitwise fashion, a composite string is generated that uniquely identifies a geographic point. This string can then be easily stored or used to transmit location point data.

Since the latitude and longitude are interleaved, geohashes have an unique property. As the number of characters decreases from the right side of the string, the accuracy decreases. Points that share similar prefixes will be close together. However, though points can be on the edge of a Geohash bounding box, not all nearby points will share similar prefixes. Since geohashes are easily stored and indexed as strings, in environments and datastores that don't have strong spatial indexing support, geohashes can be used.

The special handling of proximity queries for points on the edge of a Geohash bounding box can be compensated for by doing lookups and queries of the surrounding Geohash bounding boxes.

 MongoDB uses geohashing for its spatial queries. CouchDB however, does not. It uses R-Tree indexing, which is more flexible in terms of the type of geometries that can be indexed. This will be discussed further in the next chapter.

For more information about how the Geohash algorithm works, see the Wikipedia explanation: *http://en.wikipedia.org/wiki/Geohash*.

There are further uses of geohashing besides using it as a quick means of implementing proximity searches where only string indexing is available. A geohashed location can be used as an identifier.

A quick example of using Geohash in an application is to use it for shortened URLs. The node geohash module handles decoding geohashes, and then some Node.js code will display a Google map of the correct latitude and longitude.

The geohash module can quickly be installed using the node package manager, npm:

```
hostname $ npm install geohash
```

Here is a quick project to show an example usage of geohashes. The project will provide a URL that references a specific point on a map. Latitude and Longitude could be used in the URL, but in order to keep the URLs a little shorter, the example will use geohashes.

The example project uses ExpressJS again, as was introduced in Chapter 1, along with the geohash module that was just installed:

```
var express = require("express"),
    app = express.createServer(),
    geohash = require("geohash").GeoHash;
```

The route uses an id variable match for all the characters at the start of the path. The next step is to use the geohash module to decode the geohash captured from the URL. The decode function returns an array of three values for latitude and longitude each. The first two values are a bounding box for the geohash, based on it's precision. The third value is the point in the center of the bounds. The third value will be used to center the map.

In order to make use of the precision of the geohash, it can be used to control the inital zoom level of the map. If the geohash is longer and thus more precise, the zoom level will be closer to the ground:

```
app.get('/:id', function(req, res){
        var latlon = geohash.decodeGeoHash(req.params['id']);
        lat = latlon.latitude[2];
        lon = latlon.longitude[2];
        zoom = req.params["id"].length+2;

        res.render('index.ejs', { layout: false, lat:lat, lon:lon, zoom:zoom,
            geohash:req.params['id']});
});

app.listen(8000);
```

After the parameters are set up, the render function is passed those parameters, which then calls the simple index.ejs template. Then the location of the geohash will be shown using Google Maps.

```
<html>
  <head>
    <title>GeoHash</title>
    <script type="text/javascript"
          src="http://maps.google.com/maps/api/js?sensor=true"></script>
    <script type="text/javascript">
      var loadMap = function(){
          var myLatlng = new google.maps.LatLng( <%= lat %>, <%= lon %>);
          var myOptions = {
              zoom: <%= zoom %>,
              center: myLatlng,
              mapTypeId: google.maps.MapTypeId.ROADMAP
          };
          map = new google.maps.Map(document.getElementById("map"), myOptions);
      };
      window.onload = loadMap;
    </script>
  </head>
  <body>
    <h2>Geohash: <%= geohash %></h2>
    <div id="map" style="width:500px;height:500px;"></div>
  </body>
</html>
```

A live example of this can be seen at *http://geohash.mapchat.im/* and all the code can be found at *http://github.com/dthompson/example_geohash_to_location*

Being able to convert and parse geospatial data is a big step towards more complex applications. There are several options available for storing geospatial data—Geocouch is a great choice.

CHAPTER 3

CouchDB

CouchDB started as a document store with the great ability to replicate data between nodes. This makes it ideal for use cases that involve eventual or relaxed consistency. The built-in replication also makes it the ideal platform for synchronization between mobile, desktop and server. CouchDB sports no fixed schema. Instead it stores documents which are formatted in JSON. JSON, being a lightweight and easy-to-understand notation for simple data structures, is great for this task. And without a rigid schema, CouchDB excels at being a fast developer-friendly datastore.

How Does CouchDB Work?

CouchDB is eventually consistent. CAP Theorem states that any database can only have two out of three of the core properties of a data store. These are:

- Consistency: That all database clients see the same copy of the data.
- Availability: that all database clients are able to access a version of the data.
- Partition tolerance: That the database can be split over multiple servers.

Since CouchDB's focus is on being partition-tolerant and highly available, this means it is eventually consistent.

Replication

CouchDB's built in replication can be super useful in creating a highly available and partition tolerant system. Locally, CouchDB uses MVCC (Multi-Version Concurrency Control) to provide consistent access to data. This means that versions of documents are stored, and updates are appended. Read requests can always read from the most recent version of the document with no need for locking on write requests. Versioning is also important in replication between servers.

Incremental replication is used to keep multiple CouchDB servers in sync. Changes are periodically copied between servers. This does not have to be a one way operation like the classic master/slave setup that is commonly used by other databases. CouchDB handles conflict detection and resolution. When a conflict on a document is detected, it is flagged as being conflicted. The automatic resolution picks a winning copy of the document (the most recent one) and saves the losing version as well. This happens consistently on both servers. If this automatic resolution is not advanced enough for the needs of the application conflicts can be resolved by the application in a why that makes sense. The application can leave the winning document in place, choose the other version that was saved to the history of the document, or create a new merged version of the document.

Indexes and Views

Lookups in CouchDB are all key based. In fact the core storage engine used in CouchDB is a B-tree. B-trees are an efficient sorted data structure. Using this allows CouchDB to quickly perform lookups on keys. This same storage engine is used for documents is also used for generated views. This means that querying a view in CouchDB can be very fast. In order to create a view, CouchDB uses MapReduce functions written in Java-Script.

MapReduce is used to compute the results of a view. These views are updated according to changes to documents stored by CouchDB automatically when views are requested.

Getting Started with CouchDB

The easiest way to get started using CouchDB for development is by downloading and installing a build of Couchbase. Builds are available for most major operating systems at *http://www.couchbase.com/downloads*.

Couchbase is a company that combines the power and utility of CouchDB with Membase. Several of the core committers to the Apache CouchDB project work at Couchbase. They also offer CouchDB hosting options at Iris Couch (*http://www.iriscouch .com/*).

After installing Couchbase, run it. The built-in administrator console, Futon, can be found at the default URL, *http://127.0.0.1:5984/_utils/*.

Futon is a full database management interface for CouchDB. Futon can create and delete databases, setup replication, and even design and test views. Futon is built on the same HTTP API that is used by clients to talk to the database.

Creating a Database

Futon includes the ability to create new databases and add some initial data. When adding a new document, CouchDB already adds an ID to the document automatically. The ID is added to the document as the special property "_id". This ID can be modified, but it does need to be unique for the entire database. After saving the document CouchDB will add another special property, "_rev". The "_rev" property is used to track multiple revisions of a document. Futon includes links to "Previous Version" and "Next Version" on the document page. Past revisions of documents can be viewed once there have been changes saved to the document.

Add some sample data. The sample document will describe a person with the properties name, age, and gender. The document should look something like this:

```
{
    "_id": "618f6d552f8cf3061934a4d08700089a",
    "_rev": "1-a9f8690408bbffaf3389dc1aa5ecd79c",
    "name": "John",
    "age": 23,
    "gender": "male"
}
```

Create two more entries of the person document so there is enough data to show some example CouchDB views:

```
{
    "_id": "618f6d552f8cf3061934a4d087000d55",
    "_rev": "1-06b9a4a10fc3d2dc062d310d7cd28b59",
    "name": "Jane",
    "age": 24,
    "gender": "female"
}

{
    "_id": "618f6d552f8cf3061934a4d087001098",
    "_rev": "1-665db2e1bea428152881189c24400739",
    "name": "Jim",
    "age": 21,
    "gender": "male"
}
```

Creating a View

Views use map reduce in order to generate a list of documents. The first example will be of a Map only View. In the Futon view drop-down, select "Temporary view". This is a convenient way of writing and testing views.

 Views are designed to be caluated ahead of time and update incrementally. Keep the test dataset small so the temporary view won't take long to run. This helps when you are testing many changes quickly.

First, here's a really simple view:

```
function(doc) {
  if(doc.gender == "male"){
    emit(doc.age, doc);
  }
}
```

The map function of the view selects what documents to add to the view, what fields to use as the index, and what data to output for the corresponding document. In this case the function will only add documents that have a gender property set equal to "male". Then the age property will be used as the key to index.

Run the view to make sure CouchDB returns the correct results. There should be two results: Jim and John. Their ages, 21 and 23, should be used as the key.

Save this temporary view to create a permanent view. If it is the first time the view is saved, then choose "Save as" and enter a filename. Views are saved in design documents, so they need both a name for the design document and the view. For this example, use "person" as the design document and "males" as the view.

Assuming the name of the database is "example," the URL of the view is *http://127.0.0.1:5984/example/_design/person/_view/males*.

This is the JSON result of the view:

```
{
    "total_rows": 2,
    "offset": 0,
    "rows": [
        {
            "id": "618f6d552f8cf3061934a4d087001098",
            "key": 21,
            "value": {
                "_id": "618f6d552f8cf3061934a4d087001098",
                "_rev": "1-665db2e1bea428152881189c24400739",
                "name": "Jim",
                "age": 21,
                "gender": "male"
            }
        },
        {
            "id": "618f6d552f8cf3061934a4d08700089a",
            "key": 23,
            "value": {
                "_id": "618f6d552f8cf3061934a4d08700089a",
                "_rev": "1-a9f8690408bbffaf3389dc1aa5ecd79c",
                "name": "John",
                "age": 23,
                "gender": "male"
            }
        }
    ]
}
```

View Options

Once views are generated there are several query options that can be added to the URL as parameters. URL parameters control offsets, limit the number of rows returned, find individual keys, and even group by key.

In order to limit the rows, the view returns to a single row, so set the limit parameter:

http://127.0.0.1:5984/example/_design/person/_view/males?limit=1

This outputs:

```
{
    "total_rows": 2,
    "offset": 0,
    "rows": [
        {
            "id": "618f6d552f8cf3061934a4d087001098",
            "key": 21,
            "value": {
                "_id": "618f6d552f8cf3061934a4d087001098",
                "_rev": "1-665db2e1bea428152881189c24400739",
                "name": "Jim",
                "age": 21,
                "gender": "male"
            }
        }
    ]
}
```

Notice that CouchDB still returns the total number of rows in the view, and the offset of where the rows begin.

Skipping one row will return the next row—John age 23:

http://127.0.0.1:5984/example/_design/person/_view/males?limit=1&skip=1

This outputs:

```
{
    "total_rows": 2,
    "offset": 1,
    "rows": [
        {
            "id": "618f6d552f8cf3061934a4d08700089a",
            "key": 23,
            "value": {
                "_id": "618f6d552f8cf3061934a4d08700089a",
                "_rev": "1-a9f8690408bbffaf3389dc1aa5ecd79c",
                "name": "John",
                "age": 23,
                "gender": "male"
            }
        }
    ]
}
```

Using these simple limit and skip parameters, combined with offset and total_row properties of the returned JSON response, it is super easy to set up paging for a set of rows in a view. A full list of parameters that can be included in the view request are in Table 3-1.

Table 3-1. CouchDB View Options

Parameter	Value	Default	Description
key	key-value	-	URL encoded JSON value
startkey	key-value	-	URL encoded JSON value
startkey_docid	document id	-	The starting document ID
endkey	key-value	-	URL encoded JSON value
endkey_docid	document id	-	The ending document ID
limit	number	-	The number of documents to return (rows)
stale	"ok"/"update_after"	-	Specifies if it is OK to return a stale view for the request. Leave this out and it will be generated before returning a response.
descending	"true"/"false"	false	Reverses the rows (sorted by keys)
skip	number	0	Skips this number of documents.
group	"true"/"false"	false	Groups by key (this reduces rows to distinct keys).
group_level	number	-	Specifies how many parts of the key to consider in compound keys when grouping.
reduce	"true"/"false"	true	Specifies whether to run the reduce function on the view.
include_docs	"true"/"false"	false	Automatically fetches the document for each row and include it in the JSON response.
inclusive_end	"true"/"false"	true	Specifies whether the endkey is included in the result.

Using Reduce

The view examples so far have just used map functions. Using a reduce function in the view adds the ability to create aggregate results. reduce functions have to accept two different inputs: results emitted from the map function and results that are returned from the reduce function itself:

```
function (keys, values, rereduce) {
    return sum(values);
}
```

The reduce function is passed three arguments: keys, which are an array of key and document ID pairs; values, which are either the values emitted from the map function, or are values that get returned from prior runs of the reduce function; and the third argument, rereduce, which will be false if the values are from the map function and true if they are results of the reduce function.

There are two cases to handle in a reduce function. The first is when the values come from data emitted by the map function:

```
reduce([ [key1,id1], [key2,id2], [key3,id3] ], [value1,value2,value3], false)
```

The second case is when the values come from previous runs of the reduce function:

```
reduce(null, [reduceResult, reduceResult, reduceResult], true)
```

Most of the time the best way to deal with this is to emit from the map function and return from the reduce function the same values.

 When things go wrong in a view, it is sometimes hard to tell what is happening. Keeping views small and simple as well as keeping your dataset small can help, but sometimes you need to debug output. The log() function is built into CouchDB and will log a string value to CouchDB.log. Check the install documentation for the platform to see where the log file is placed on the system.

Using CouchApps...For Fun and Profit

CouchApps is a simple way of writing JS/HTML applications that are hosting completely on CouchDB. They serve up all static files from CouchDB, use CouchDB as a data store, and include easy ways to replicate these apps or just the data they contain. Find out more at *http://couchapp.org/*.

Beyond just standalone apps in CoucbDB, some of the tools for CouchApps can be super useful for creating and managing views, lists, and shared JS files. The CouchApp command tool can be used to push view functions to a CouchDB database based on a file structure. This makes it easier to edit views in a text editor and still keep those changes in sync.

CouchApp tools can be found on github at *https://github.com/couchapp/couchapp*.

After installing CouchApp, create a new CouchApp project. This will generate the file structure for the CouchApp. The name of the CouchApp is used as the name of a design document that will contain the views:

```
hostname $ couchapp generate people
```

This will create the directory named *people* with the following files:

```
hostname $ ls -l people/
total 32
-rw-r--r--  1 thompson  thompson  1660 Jan  9 18:12 README.md
drwxr-xr-x  4 thompson  thompson   136 Jun 17 08:43 _attachments
-rw-r--r--  1 thompson  thompson    14 Jun 17 08:43 _id
-rw-r--r--  1 thompson  thompson    70 Jan  9 18:12 couchapp.json
drwxr-xr-x  4 thompson  thompson   136 Jun 17 08:43 evently
-rw-r--r--  1 thompson  thompson    10 Jan  9 18:12 language
drwxr-xr-x  2 thompson  thompson    68 Jun 17 08:43 lists
drwxr-xr-x  2 thompson  thompson    68 Jun 17 08:43 shows
```

```
drwxr-xr-x  2 thompson  thompson   68 Jun 17 08:43 updates
drwxr-xr-x  3 thompson  thompson  102 Jun 17 08:43 vendor
drwxr-xr-x  3 thompson  thompson  102 Jun 17 08:43 views
```

The files here are going to be pushed into a design document in CouchDB. All the directories and files here will be converted into a JSON representation. The directory names will be used as names of arrays that contain key value pairs of filenames and file contents.

From inside the new *people* directory, add a view:

```
couchapp generate view age
```

That will create a directory named *age* in the views directory that contains two files: *map.js* and *reduce.js*. Those files will contain stubbed functions for map and reduce of the age view. Edit the map so it emits ages for each person (views/age/map.js):

```
function(doc) {
    emit(doc.name, doc.age);
}
```

Then in the reduce function, sum all of those ages (views/age/reduce.js):

```
function(keys, values, rereduce) {
    return sum(values);
}
```

CouchApp defaults to pushing to your localhost at CouchDB's standard port. Just push to the example database from before:

```
hostname $ couchapp push example
```

Now, the result of the new MapReduce view can be seen here: *http://127.0.0.1:5984/example/_design/people/_view/age*:

```
{
    "rows": [
        {
            "key": null,
            "value": 68
        }
    ]
}
```

The value is 68, the sum of all the ages in the database.

Load Shared Code

CouchDB allows the loading of JavaScript files into a view. This is helpful when including a lot of code, or a library that is used by multiple views. First, add some code to the vendor directory. Then, load that in a map function (vendor/timing.js):

```
/*
 * This creates a timing object that has a shared function for our views
 */
```

```
var timing = {};

timing.YearToSeconds = function(years){
    var curDate = new Date();
    var startDate = (new Date());
    startDate.setFullYear(curDate.getFullYear() - years);

    return (curDate.getTime() - startDate.getTime()) /1000;
};
```

CouchApp supports using macros to load shared code in place before sending it to CouchDB. Create a new view to load this JavaScript file and use the YearToSeconds function to add seconds to the response. The new view can be named ageByYear.

```
hostname $ couchapp generate view ageByYear
```

This creates the directory for the view with the *map.js* and *reduce.js* files. There is no need for a reduce function in this example, so the *reduce.js* file can be deleted so that the reduce function will not be run.

In the *map.js* file, the function is set up to include the shared code:

```
function(doc) {

    // Next line is CouchApp directive
    // !code vendor/timing.js
    emit(doc.name, {
            "age":
                {
                    "seconds": timing.YearToSeconds(doc.age),
                    "age": doc.age
                }
        });
}
```

The directive in the comment is seen by CouchApp and replaced with the contents of the specified file. This allows sharing code between views. In other CouchDB functions such as show, list, and update, modules can be loaded in the same fashion as CommonJS. This is also the same way modules are loaded in Node.js. There are differences in the JavaScript interpreter used by CouchDB and Node.js, including several functions that are not supported in both environments. However, some simple modules can be shared between Node.js and CouchDB.

Again, push these changes to CouchDB using couchapp:

```
hostname $ couchapp push example
```

The new view can be requested at *http://127.0.0.1:5984/example/_design/people/_view/ageByYear*.

The output now includes both the person's age in years and in seconds for all documents:

```
{
    "total_rows": 3,
    "offset": 0,
    "rows": [
        {
            "id": "618f6d552f8cf3061934a4d087000d55",
            "key": "Jane",
            "value": {
                "age": {
                    "seconds": 757382400,
                    "age": 24
                }
            }
        },
        {
            "id": "618f6d552f8cf3061934a4d087001098",
            "key": "Jim",
            "value": {
                "age": {
                    "seconds": 662688000,
                    "age": 21
                }
            }
        },
        {
            "id": "618f6d552f8cf3061934a4d08700089a",
            "key": "John",
            "value": {
                "age": {
                    "seconds": 725760000,
                    "age": 23
                }
            }
        }
    ]
}
```

For more information about the CouchDB view API and the options that are available, the CouchDB wiki is a great resource: *http://wiki.apache.org/couchdb/HTTP_view_API*.

GeoCouch

GeoCouch is an branch of CouchDB that was created by Volker Mische. Within the same RESTful view framework of CouchDB he added a new index, R-trees. R-tree indices are used by many to store geospatial data because of speed of lookups. R-trees are basically a collection of bounding boxes—or ranges—that contain pointers to actual points in that range or other sub ranges contained in the parent range. This reduces the number of bounding boxes that need to be queried, as the dataset can most often be limited to a much smaller subset of the points stored. GeoCouch was merged and released as part of the new Couchbase, a merged datastore with functionality from both CouchDB and Membase. GeoCouch offers an easy way to build spatial indices by simply including GeoJSON formatted geometry data in the CouchDB view.

Importing Data

In order to start exploring the functionality that GeoCouch adds, we need to import some data. The next example uses a list of 500 geotagged photos fetched from the Flickr API.

The code for importing the data from Flickr to CouchDB, the view functions as a couchapp project, and the data itself can be found on github: *https://github.com/dthompson/example_geocouch_data*.

The data was gathered from Flickr using this request. To update the data, just get a free API key from Flickr and include it with the request:

```
http://api.flickr.com/services/rest/?method=flickr.photos.search&api_key=
    <API_KEY>&text=kitty+cat&has_geo=true&extras=geo&per_page=1000&
    format=json&nojsoncallback=1
```

JSON Response:

```
{ "photos": { "page": 1, "pages": "116", "perpage": "500", "total": "57870",
    "photo": [
      { "id": "5845159255", "owner": "11032335@N00", "secret": "4f81b07060",
        "server": "2778", "farm": 3, "title": "Wolfie enjoys his carpet tunnel",
        "ispublic": 1, "isfriend": 0, "isfamily": 0, "latitude": 37.33847,
        "longitude": -121.885787, "accuracy": 11, "place_id": "BG4MINxTVrLjdwou",
        "woeid": "2488042", "geo_is_family": 0, "geo_is_friend": 0,
        "geo_is_contact": 0, "geo_is_public": 1 },
      ....

    ] }, "stat": "ok" }
```

Using Cradle to Talk to Geocouch

In order to import the data into CouchDB, the data needs to read from the file, parsed, a couple extra properties need to be added to the dictionary, and then saved that to CouchDB. The script uses the cradle node module to interact with CouchDB.

Currently, Cradle does not support spatial views. Spatial view support has been added to my fork of cradle on github at *https://github.com/dthompson/cradle*. Either grab the commit that adds spatial view support, use the dthompson fork, or check to see if a spatial function has been added to the main cradle repository.

Cradle can be installed from npm:

```
hostname $ npm install cradle
```

Now it's time to import the data from Flickr's JSON response. The script imports to the localhost in a database named geoexample.

```
var cradle = require("cradle"),
    sys = require("sys"),
    fs = require("fs");

var connection = new(cradle.Connection)("localhost", 5984);
var db = connection.database('geoexample');

data = fs.readFileSync("flickr_data.json", "utf-8");

flickr = JSON.parse(data);

for(p in flickr.photos.photo){
    photo = flickr.photos.photo[p];

    photo.geometry = {"type":"Point",
                      "coordinates": [photo.longitude, photo.latitude]};

    // Save the URL to the Flickr image.
    // http://farm{farm-id}.static.flickr.com/{server-id}/{id}_{secret}_[mstzb].jpg

    photo.image_url_small = "http://farm"+photo.farm+".static.flickr.com/"+
        photo.server+"/"+photo.id+"_"+photo.secret+"_s.jpg";

    db.save(photo.id, photo, function(er, ok) {
            if (er) {sys.puts("error: "+er); return;}
        });
}
```

Add the Couchapp

Now that there is some example data in CouchDB, the next thing to do is add a spatial view. Again, use couchapp to sync the local view files to CouchDB. The new example CouchApp is named geocats:

```
hostname $couchapp generate geocats
```

CouchApp does not generate the spatial views, so they need to added. Create a directory named *spatial* inside the CouchApp. Inside the *spatial* directory is where the spatial views will be added. Unlike normal views in CouchDB, spatial views do not support MapReduce. Currently the views are just a single map function (geocats/spatial/points.js):

```
function(doc) {
    if(doc.geometry){
        emit(doc.geometry, {image:doc.image_url_small});
    }
}
```

The emit function in spatial views requires the key to be a geometry in valid GeoJSON format. The output can be Points, Polylines, Polygons, etc. This example outputs the geometry of the point where the photo was taken. The valid GeoJSON is saved in the document on import, but it can also be constructed inside the view function as well.

Bounding Box Queries

Now that the spatial view function is outputting the geometry, CouchDB will create a R-tree index for queries against the geospatial data. The results can been seen here: *http://127.0.0.1:5984/geoexample/_design/geocats/_spatial/points?bbox=-0,0,180,90.*

This will return results for the bounding box 0,0 180,90 or half the globe.

This is the JSON response from CouchDB:

```
{
    "update_seq": 508,
    "rows": [
        {
            "id": "5807724052",
            "bbox": [
                -157.964782,
                21.4836,
                -157.964782,
                21.4836
            ],
            "geometry": {
                "type": "Point",
                "coordinates": [
                    -157.964782,
                    21.4836
                ]
            },
            "value": {
                "image":
                "http://farm3.static.flickr.com/2646/5807724052_9f7b947da9_s.jpg"
            }
        }
        //...MORE ROWS...
    ]
}
```

Valid GeoJSON geometry is included in the response, along with the bounds or bbox that contains the geometry. The value property is the second argument that is passed to the emit function. It can be any value—in this case, the function is returning the URL to the photo on Flickr.

Displaying the Data Using Node.js

Since the points are now being returned, and a bounds can be set to only return what is needed to be displayed, make a quick map display for this data. Set up a simple Node.js app to serve up the map and proxy requests to CouchDB:

```
var express = require("express"),
    app = express.createServer(),
    cradle = require("cradle"),
    sys = require("sys");

var connection = new(cradle.Connection)("localhost", 5984);
var db = connection.database('geoexample');

app.get('/geocats', function(req, res){
        bbox = req.param('bbox');
        db.spatial("geocats/points",
                    {"bbox":bbox, "descending": "true"},
                    function(er, docs) {
                        if(er){sys.puts("Error: "+sys.inspect(er));
                            res.send("error");return;}
                        res.send(docs);
                    });
    });

app.get('/', function(req, res){
        res.render('index.ejs', { layout: false});
    });

app.listen(8000);
```

There are two simple routes. The first one, geocats, serves up the CouchDB data for bounding box queries. The second route just serves up the main page template.

The Google Maps client code will take into account the bounds map when requesting points from CouchDB. It will also re-request points once the user changes the bounds of the map. Bounds changes will happen when the user zooms the map, or moves the center of the map.

The bounds_changed event will be used to know then the map bounds have been adjusted. Google Maps uses the order latitude, longtiude and so do a few other map libraries. But GeoJSON, along with many server side geospatial libraries, orders points as longitude, latitude. The client code has to take this into account in a couple places:

```
google.maps.event.addListener(map, 'bounds_changed', function() {
    bounds = map.getBounds();

    // We'll make our own bounding box string, so it is in the order CouchDB expects
    bbox = [bounds.getSouthWest().lng(),bounds.getSouthWest().lat(),
            bounds.getNorthEast().lng(),bounds.getNorthEast().lat()];

    $.get("/geocats?bbox="+bbox.join(","), function(data){
        count = 0;
```

```
        for(d in data){
            row = data[d];

            // Note that we also reverse the order of the coordinates returned from
            // CouchDB when displaying them on the map
            myLatlng = new google.maps.LatLng(row.geometry.coordinates[1],
                                            row.geometry.coordinates[0]);
            var marker = new google.maps.Marker({
                position: myLatlng,
                map: map,
                title:"cat"
            });
        }
    });
});
```

To round out the example, we will add the ability to click on a point and see the photo from that location. We can use an Google Maps infowindow to show that picture. The complete display code is below:

```
<html>
  <head>
    <title>GeoCats</title>
    <script type="text/javascript"
        src="http://maps.google.com/maps/api/js?sensor=true"></script>
    <script type="text/javascript"
        src="https://ajax.googleapis.com/ajax/libs/jquery/1.6.1/jquery.min.js">
        </script>
    <script type="text/javascript">
      var map = {};
      var markers = [];
      var infowindows = [];
      var loadMap = function(){
          if(navigator.geolocation) {
              navigator.geolocation.getCurrentPosition(function(position) {
                  initialLocation = new google.maps.LatLng(position.coords.latitude,
                                      position.coords.longitude);
                  map.setCenter(initialLocation);
              });
          }
          var myLatlng = new google.maps.LatLng(39.7071, -100.4589);
          var myOptions = {
              zoom: 5,
              center: myLatlng,
              mapTypeId: google.maps.MapTypeId.ROADMAP
          };
          var addInfoWindow = function(image, marker){
              contentString = "<img src='"+image+"' />";
              var infowindow = new google.maps.InfoWindow({
                  content: contentString,
                  disableAutoPan: true
              });
              infowindows.push(infowindow);
```

```
                google.maps.event.addListener(marker, 'click', function() {
                    for(i in infowindows){ infowindows[i].close();}
                    infowindow.open(map,this);
                });
            };

            map = new google.maps.Map(document.getElementById("map"), myOptions);
            google.maps.event.addListener(map, 'bounds_changed', function() {
                bounds = map.getBounds();
                bbox = [bounds.getSouthWest().lng(),bounds.getSouthWest().lat(),
                        bounds.getNorthEast().lng(),bounds.getNorthEast().lat()];
                $.get("/geocats?bbox="+bbox.join(","), function(data){
                    for(m in markers){markers[m].setMap(null);}
                    markers = [];
                    count = 0;
                    for(d in data){
                        row = data[d];
                        myLatlng = new google.maps.LatLng(row.geometry.coordinates[1],
                                                row.geometry.coordinates[0]);
                        var marker = new google.maps.Marker({
                            position: myLatlng,
                            map: map,
                            title:"cat"
                          });
                        addInfoWindow(row.value.image, marker);
                        markers.push(marker);
                        count++;
                    }
                });
            });
        };
        window.onload = loadMap;
    </script>
  </head>
  <body>
    <h2>Cats on a Map</h2>
    <div id="map" style="width:100%;height:500px;"></div>
  </body>
</html>
```

CouchDB can be used to quickly store geospatial data and use spatial indexing, to allow return of only the points that are currently visible to the user. This is helpful for reducing the amount of data that needs to be sent to the user, and the number of points that the map needs to render at one time. This makes the map fast and easy to use. The data can be seen on a map, as in Figure 3-1.

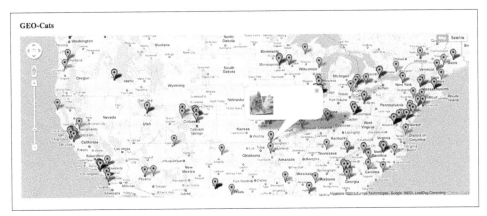

Figure 3-1. Display CouchDB Data using Google Maps

CouchDB Hosting Options

CouchDB is a well maintained project that has easy-to-use build scripts. Getting a CouchDB packaged for specific OSs is also an option. However, sometimes it is easier not having host CouchDB at all. There are a couple of CouchDB hosting options.

Cloudant (*http://cloudant.com*) was one of the first companies to focus on hosted CouchDB. They offer free options for a limited sized dataset as well as a limited number of requests. Their focus is on hosting large size datasets in CouchDB. They have developed Big Couch (*https://cloudant.com/solutions/bigcouch*) which added distributing dataset over multiple servers. This allows CouchDB to handle much larger sizes of databases.

IrisCouch is run by Couchbase, and involves several of the core committers to CouchDB. This hosting service is a bit new, but easy to sign up for and get started with. They are currently the only provider of hosted GeoCouch functionality. The quickest way to get CouchDB that that includes spatial indexing is IrisCouch.

CHAPTER 4

MapChat - Example Project

Node.js has made it simple to run event code on the web, as well as perform some basic geospatial operations. CouchDB gives a quick easy way to query spatial indices as well as a robust document based data store. Combined, these tools can be used to easily create a great new project.

The project is *www.mapchat.im*. It will allow users to interact by posting real-time chat messages that are tagged with their current location on the map. Other users will see only the messages that are in their current map bounds. CouchDB will be used to store history for the map chat room, and will also handle server side point clustering so multiple chat messages in the same area will be grouped into a conversations. The project will include several other smaller features, including using a custom Google Maps overlay to display chat messages.

Realtime Chat

There are many chat examples for Node.js. Some of the more interesting Node.js projects leverage websockets where available and use JSON to exchange data quickly, giving the developer a synchronized object that both the client- and server-side JavaScript can use. XHR-long polling is also a technique used in order to provide information about changes from the server or client quickly, even in older browsers. One project has become in many ways the standard for real-time communication between the browser and the server: socket.io.

Socket.io

Socket.io provides a simple API for an application to use to handle messages passing between the client and server. It automatically uses the best type of connection available. That includes using websockets, flash proxy, XHR-long polling, and a few others. Many of the other libraries such as now.js are built on top of the functionality of socket.io. Socket.io has proven to be such a good idea that it has been ported to a couple of other server side languages, though Node.js surely has the most consistent feel between the client and server API.

Install Socket.io using the Node.js Package Manager:

```
npm install socket.io
```

To get started, look at a simple example of using socket.io to pass messages back and forth. The server first needs to start up a socket.io listener:

```
var io = require('socket.io').listen(80);

io.sockets.on('connection', function (socket) {
    socket.send({message:"hello"});
});
```

After setting up the socket.io object, a callback is added for new connections. Once the callback is run, it sends the client a JavaScript object.

On the client side, it loads the socket.io JavaScript, and then connects to the server:

```
<script src="/socket.io/socket.io.js"></script>
<script>
  var socket = io.connect('http://localhost');
  socket.on('message', function (data) {
    console.log(data);
  });
</script>
```

When the client gets a new message, which will happen when it first connects, the client will output the message to the browser console log.

Setting Up the Project

MapChat uses the ExpressJS web framework. Socket.io handles all of its own setup; it just needs to be passed the server object which is returned by the createServer function:

```
var express = require("express"),
    app = express.createServer(),
    io = require("socket.io");

socket = io.listen(app);
```

It is that simple to set up socket.io to work with ExpressJS.

Now to set up the rest of the web app. The application will need to serve some static files for the JavaScript and stylesheet as well as a couple of images. To do this, add a static handler. Everything on a path that starts with "/static" will be served from a directory named "static" in the root of our application directory:

```
app.use('/static', express.static(__dirname + '/static'));
```

Now add the handler for the main page:

```
app.get('/', function(req, res){
    res.render('index.ejs', { layout: false});
});
```

This looks for the view template "index.ejs" in the "views" directory. The view template is fairly simple:

```
<html>
  <head>
    <title>Map Chat</title>
    <script type="text/javascript"
     src="https://ajax.googleapis.com/ajax/libs/jquery/1.5.2/jquery.min.js"></script>
    <script type="text/javascript" src="/socket.io/socket.io.js"></script>
    <script type="text/javascript"
     src="http://maps.google.com/maps/api/js?sensor=true"></script>
    <script type="text/javascript" src="/static/client.js"></script>
    <link rel="stylesheet" type="text/css" href="/static/style.css" />
  </head>
  <body>
    <div id="content">
      <div id="headerwrapper">
        <div id="header">
          <div id="logo">
          </div>
        </div>
      </div>
      <div id="footerwrapper">
        <div id="chatsend">
          <div id="chatarea"><textarea id="message"></textarea></div>
          <div id="send">
            Send
          </div>
        </div>
      </div>
      <div id="map"></div>
    </div>
  </body>
</html>
```

The JavaScript that gets loaded is for jQuery, socket.io, which is automatically served by socket.io, Google Maps, and our own client JavaScript. There is also a stylesheet. The stylesheet is basic, but can be altered to change most of the application's style. It is included in the example code for MapChat.

Now the application is ready for the server to start listening for user requests.

```
app.listen(8000);
```

Making chat subscriptions

Socket.io will form the basis for messaging between the client and server in MapChat. After the connection is created, the client will make a subscription request to the server which will include the client's current map bounds. In the JavaScript after socket.io is set up, pass the hardcoded data for a worldwide subscription:

```
bounds = [[-180,-90],[180, 90]];
socket.send({action:"subscribe", bounds:bounds});
```

When the server gets a new subscription message from the client, it will add the client along with its bounds to the subscription list:

```
mapchat = {
    subscriptions: [],
    subscribe:function(client, msg){

        bottomlatlng = new geojs.latLng(msg.bounds[0][1], msg.bounds[0][0]);
        toplatlng = new geojs.latLng(msg.bounds[1][1], msg.bounds[1][0]);
        bounds = new geojs.bounds(bottomlatlng, toplatlng);

        var allReadySubscribed = false;

        // If this connection already has a subscription update the bounds
        for(s in mapchat.subscriptions){
            if(mapchat.subscriptions[s].client.sessionId == client.sessionId){
                allReadySubscribed = true;

                //Set new bounds.
                mapchat.subscriptions[s].bounds = bounds
                break;
            }
        }

        // If no existing subscription, then add a new one.
        if(!allReadySubscribed){
            mapchat.subscriptions.push({client:client,
                                        bounds:bounds});
        }
    }
};
```

When a client connects and sends a subscription, we add it to the subscription list. But first the application checks to see if the connection already has a subscription, and if there is an existing subscription, it updates the new bounds. Subscription information does not need to be persisted so it is just kept in memory.

There needs to be a handler for the subscription messages from the client. The client adds the property named action and sets that to subscribe, so the server knows how to handle that message:

```
socket.on('connection', function(client){
    client.on('message', function(msg){
        if(msg.action == "subscribe"){
            mapchat.subscribe(this, msg);
```

```
        }else if(msg.action="message"){
            mapchat.message(this,msg);
        }
    });
});
```

On a new connection on the server, there needs to be a handler for new messages from the client. Then the server can check the `action` property that the client added and handle the messages properly.

Socket.io has just added handling for custom event names. Using the `emit` function instead of send, the client can name the event that the message will trigger on the server or vice versa. The server or client can add a callback for that event using the same "on" function and specifying the event name as the first argument.

Handling Chat Messages

Now that the server has a subscription set up, the client can send a message. The client will send the chat message tagged with the current center of the map. For now, start by just sending a message with a hardcoded location:

```
var lat = 40.334,
    lon -103.644;
var point = {"type":"Point", "coordinates":[lon, lat]};
socket.send({action:"message", message:"hello",  geometry:point});
```

On the server, the messages from the client will be handled by checking the action property, and when that is set to "message", calling the `message` function:

```
mapchat = {

    //subscribe: function...,

    message: function(client, msg){

        // Save message to the database
        msg.date = new Date();
        db.save(msg, function (err, res) {
            if(err){sys.puts("error: "+sys.inspect(err));}
        });

        for(s in mapchat.subscriptions){
            sub = mapchat.subscriptions[s];

            // We dont need to send a message to the same client that
            // sent the message.
            if(sub.client.sessionId != client.sessionId){

                // Check see if the bounds match.
                point = new geojs.point(msg.geometry);
                if(sub.bounds.contains(point)){
                    sub.client.send({"type":"message",
```

```
                               "geometry":msg.geometry,
                               "message":msg.message});
                }
            }
        }
    }
};
```

First the new message is saved to CouchDB so that the map can prepopulated on the first load with with recent messages. Next, the subscription list is checked to see if the new message is inside the bounds of any of the existing subscriptions. If the message is inside the bounds, it will be sent to that client. The client will then show the new message on the map. For now, the client will just output the message to the console.

Depending on the browser's script console, the output of the object sent to the client should like something like this:

```
geometry: Object
    coordinates: Array[2]
        0: -105.27054499999997
        1: 40.014985
    type: "Point"
message: "hello"
type: "message"
```

Now that the messages are being successfully passed back and forth between the client and server, the client interface can be added next.

Using Google Maps

Chat messages should be shown on the map, and new messages should also be tagged with the current center of the map that the user is viewing. Google Maps is easy to use, and is what we will use for MapChat. There are other JavaScript map options, including open source projects like *http://openlayers.org/*.

Now to set up the map:

```
$(document).ready(function(){
    var myLatlng = new google.maps.LatLng(40.334, -103.644);
    var myOptions = {
        zoom: 8,
        center: myLatlng,
        mapTypeId: google.maps.MapTypeId.ROADMAP
    };
    map = new google.maps.Map(jQuery("#map")[0], myOptions);
});
```

This will simply default the map to a hardcoded location and load it at zoom level 8. To make MapChat more interesting to the user, it will start them out at their current location.

Getting User Location

Modern browsers allow JavaScript to request the user's current location. The browsers all then ask if the user wants to share their location with the current website. Not all of the users will allow location, nor will all browsers support it. In MapChat if the browser doesn't support returning location, or if the user does not allow it, the map will default to a central location. Another option would be to add a lookup using the user's IP address to get a general location based on the Whois record for that IP range. There are databases for this available—however they are not always accurate, especially on mobile devices. Using the built in location request in the browser is becoming more widely supported, gives a more accurate answer, and allows users to opt out of the feature if sharing their location is not something the user is comfortable allowing.

Grab browser location

In order to get the user's location, the client has to check to see if the browser supports location, and if it does, register a callback function to handle the data once the user allows it and the browser has been able to locate the user.

 The way the browser gets the location information varies. It can be a lookup of the location based on IP, based on the known location of wireless networks in the area, or on some devices, especially mobile, via GPS. All we need to know is what to do on the callback.

The code to handle browser location:

```
if(navigator.geolocation) {
    navigator.geolocation.getCurrentPosition(function(position) {
        initialLocation = new google.maps.LatLng(position.coords.latitude,
                                                  position.coords.longitude);
        map.setCenter(initialLocation);
    });
}
```

In this case once the callback is run, the map will be centered on the user's location.

Center and Bounds

MapChat needs to know the map bounds in order to send the subscription message, as well as the center of the map so chat messages can be tagged with the current location. In order to get the bounds the client will use the built in functionality of Google Maps and change the subscription message a bit.

```
google.maps.event.addListener(map, 'bounds_changed', function(){
    var mapbounds = map.getBounds();
    bounds = [[mapbounds.getSouthWest().lng(),
               mapbounds.getSouthWest().lat()],
              [mapbounds.getNorthEast().lng(),
               mapbounds.getNorthEast().lat()]];
```

```
        socket.send({action:"subscribe", bounds:bounds});
    });
```

Notice that the subscription code is inside a **bounds_changed** event on the map. Now when the user moves the map or changes the zoom level, the client can update the subscription on the server with the new bounds.

When the user sends new chat messages, the client needs to know the current center of the map so the client can add location to the data sent to the server:

```
var latlon = map.getCenter();
var lat = latlon.lat(),
    lon = latlon.lng();
var point = {"type":"Point", "coordinates":[lon, lat]};
socket.send({action:"message", message:chatmsg,  geometry:point});
```

Since the client now knows the location of the user, it can set the bounds subscription, as well as tag the message with the location it was sent from.

Custom Overlays

To start displaying some chat messages on the map, the client will use the default Google Maps infowindow. In the **receive message** function, the call to create and open an infowindow will be added:

```
var chat= {
    //sendMessage:function()...

    receiveMessage:function(data){
        latlon = new google.maps.LatLng(data.geometry.coordinates[1],
                                 data.geometry.coordinates[0]);
        infowindow = new google.maps.InfoWindow({
            content: data.message,
            disableAutoPan: true
        });
        infowindow.open(map);
    }
};
```

For MapChat, it would be great to show some custom overlays for chat messages. Using Google Maps, it isn't too hard to extend the build in OverlayView and make a custom overlay. Custom overlays can be used to show styled messages on maps, custom tile sets, or any other geographic data overlays.

The first step is to set up the new type of overlay. For MapChat, the custom overlay will be ChatOverlay. It is just a div with custom styling to make it fit in better with the rest of the look and feel for MapChat. Whatever data needs to be used by the overlay should be added as arguments to the function so it can be initialized in one call:

```
function ChatOverlay(latlon, message) {

    // Now initialize all properties.
    this._latlon = latlon;
    this._map = map;
    this._message = message;

    this._div = null;

    // Call setMap() on this overlay
    this.setMap(map);
}

ChatOverlay.prototype = new google.maps.OverlayView();
```

The overlay inherits from the Google Maps OverlayView. The custom overlay still needs to override some functions so it can show up properly. The onAdd function creates the element that is actually added to the map:

```
ChatOverlay.prototype.onAdd = function() {

    // Create a new div that will be added to the map.
    var chatbox = $("<div class='chatmsg'><div class='message'>"+
                        this._message+"</div></div>");
    chatbox.css("position", "absolute");

    // This is the reference to the div.
    this._div = chatbox;
    // Have to add it to a map pane. in this case the overlay layer.
    var panes = this.getPanes();
    panes.overlayLayer.appendChild(chatbox[0]);
};
```

onDraw is called as the map is rendered. It will be called again when the user moves the map, the zoom changes, or any other interaction that causes the Google map to redraw. Here the overlay's position can be set based on the current view options:

```
ChatOverlay.prototype.draw = function() {

    // This function is called when the map is redrawn, such as when the user
    // zooms or moves

    // To size and position the div correctly, get the projection.
    var overlayProjection = this.getProjection();

    // Convert the Lat Lon into a pixel position
    var point = overlayProjection.fromLatLngToDivPixel(this._latlon);
    var div = this._div;

    // The overlay is dynamically resized depending on zoom level to make
    // showing a lot of them not cover as much of the map
    width = 22 *(this.getMap().getZoom()/16)*10;
    height = 15 * (this.getMap().getZoom()/16)*10;
    div.css("width", width+"px");
    div.css("height", height+"px");
```

```
    // Set the poition of the div.
    div.css("left", point.x-(width/2) + 'px');
    div.css("top", point.y-height + 'px');
};
```

To remove overlays from the map, the overlay's map is set to null. When that happens, the API will call the overlay's onRemove function. Any extra cleanup should be done in the onRemove function:

```
ChatOverlay.prototype.onRemove = function() {
    this._div.remove();
    this._div = null;
};
```

Other functions can also be added. For example, the ability to show and hide the overlay are commonly added functions:

```
ChatOverlay.prototype.hide = function() {
    if (this._div) {
        this._div.hide();
    }
};

ChatOverlay.prototype.show = function() {
    if (this._div) {
        this._div.show();
    }
};
```

Now that the custom overlay is in place, MapChat will use the ChatOverlay for new chat messages. In the receive message function, make a new ChatOverlay.

```
var chat = {
    //sendMessage:function()...
    recieveMessage:function(data){
        latlon = new google.maps.LatLng(data.geometry.coordinates[1],
                                        data.geometry.coordinates[0]);
        var chatbox = new ChatOverlay(latlon, data.message, map);
        chatbox.show();
    }
};
```

That will open the new overlay when a message is received. With a bit of styling and adding some other data, the new custom overlay starts to look better, as seen in Figure 4-1.

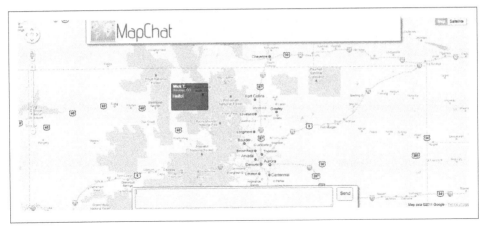

Figure 4-1. Custom Google Maps overlay

Chat Messages from CouchDB

MapChat needs to populate the map with recent messages on the first load. From CouchDB the client will get the recent messages within the current bounds of the user's subscription. This time, use the *geocouch-utils* repo to set up the spatial design document. The repository provides some extra functions for working with geospatial data in CouchDB. The repository also comes with some basic spatial view functions, which are ready to use.

The repository is available at *https://github.com/vmx/geocouch-utils*.

 There are several forks of this repo that haven't all been merged. Max Ogden has one of the most useful forks that is worth looking at for some additional functionality. The *geocouch-utils* repository includes the *geojson-js-util* repo (as a submodule) from Max. It is also available at *https://github.com/maxogden/geojson-js-utils*.

Also check out the submodule for the rep:

```
hostname $ git submodule init
hostname $ git submodule update
```

From the couchapp directory, push the geo utils to the mapchat database:

```
hostname $ couchapp push mapchat
```

If the couchapp says that it is not a valid app, then it needs a *.couchapprc* file to be added:

```
hostname $ echo "{}" > .couchapprc
```

Now from the existing chat messages, CouchDB can run spatial bounding box queries (*http://127.0.0.1:5984/mapchat/_design/geo/_spatial/points?bbox=-180,-90,180,90*).

MapChat needs more data than is returned by the default points function—and it only needs recent points. Create another spatial function (recentPoints.js):

```
function(doc){
    if(doc.geometry){
        startdate = new Date();

        //Only in the last 24hours.
        startdate.setTime(startdate.getTime() - (1000*60*60*24));
        if(doc.date > startdate){
            emit(doc.geometry, {
                id: doc._id,
                geometry: doc.geometry,
                date:doc.date,
                message:doc.message
            });
        }
    }
}
```

For new subscriptions or when the user updates their bounds, the server needs to return the recent messages in the current boundary. In the subscribe function, add a query to CouchDB:

```
mapchat = {
    subscribe:function(client, msg){

    // ...make subscription...

    bbox = bounds.toBoundsArray().join(",");
    db.spatial("geo/recentPoints", {"bbox":bbox},
        function(er, docs) {
            if(er){sys.puts("Error: "+sys.inspect(er)); return;}
            // For each of the recent message in the bounds,
            // send the client a message.
            for(d in docs){
                client.send({"type":"message",
                            "geometry":docs[d].geometry,
                            "date":docs[d].value.date,
                            "message":docs[d].value.message});
            }
        });
    }
}
```

Great! Now recent messages are loaded so when a user first gets to the map they see some past chat messages. The next feature to add is a list of the most concentrated areas of chat activity. These clusters of activity will be shown to the user as places they might want go join the conversation.

Clustering

In order to use CouchDB to cluster the points, a list function is required. List and show functions are primarily used to format data especially for use in standalone CouchApps. A list function can provide custom formatting for a view. List functions iterate over view results one row at a time, to avoid loading all the view results in the memory at once.

The *geocouch-utils* repo includes a function for proximity clustering. It works by grouping nearby points that are within a distance threshold from an averaged center point. All the list function needs to do is add documents that contain valid GeoJSON points, and it will return a list of clustered points.

Using a List Function

The proximity clustering list function is already included in *geocouch-utils*:

```
function(head, req) {

    var g = require('vendor/clustering/ProximityCluster'),
        row,
        threshold =100;

    start({"headers":{"Content-Type" : "application/json"}});
    if ('callback' in req.query) send(req.query['callback'] + "(");

    if('threshold' in req.query){ threshold = req.query.threshold;}
    var pc = new g.PointCluster(parseInt(threshold));

    while (row = getRow()) {
        pc.addToClosestCluster(row.value);
    }

    send(JSON.stringify({"rows":pc.getClusters()}));

    if ('callback' in req.query) send(")");
};
```

Three new options will be added to that list function. First, add an option to return the cluster list without the full list of points in each cluster. The cluster function, by default, includes the list of points that are included in the cluster. The second option is to sort the list by the size of each cluster. The third option is to limit the number of clusters that are returned. The call to the send function will be replaced with the following code that applies the new options:

```
// ... in the list function

clusters = pc.getClusters();
if(('nopoints' in req.query) &&(req.query.nopoints == "true")){
    for(c in clusters){
        delete clusters[c]['points'];
```

```
        }
    }
    if(('sort' in req.query) &&(req.query.sort == "true")){
        clusters.sort(function(a, b) {return a.size < b.size})
    }
    if('limit' in req.query){
        if(clusters.length >  req.query.limit){
            clusters.splice(req.query.limit, clusters.length-req.query.limit);
        }
    }
    send(JSON.stringify({"rows":clusters}));

    // ...
```

Now the new list function can be requested at *http://127.0.0.1:5984/mapchat/_design/ geo/_spatiallist/proximity-clustering/recentPoints?bbox=-180,-90,180,90&nopoints= true&sort=true&limit=2.*

Notice that this list function can be called on any view. The view to use is specified in the URL. MapChat will use the recentPoints spatial view. When querying for clustered chat locations, that data should be sent to all connected clients, as well as cached for new clients.

Notify Clients of Cluster Updates

First, add a send function to the MapChat server:

```
maphat = {
    //subscribe:function()...

    sendChatClusters: function(client){
        if(client != undefined){
            // Send to just the one client
            client.send({"type":"clusters", "clusters":mapchat.clusters});
        }else{
            // Send to all subscriptions
            for(s in mapchat.subscriptions){
                sub = mapchat.subscriptions[s];
                sub.client.send({"type":"clusters", "clusters":mapchat.clusters});
            }
        }
    }
};
```

There are two cases for this function. First, if a new client just connected, it will send them the current clustered chat locations. Second, it will periodically update all connected clients.

In mapchat.subscribe:

```
//...
if(!allReadySubscribed){
    mapchat.subscriptions.push({client:client,
                                bounds:bounds});
```

```
        mapchat.sendChatClusters(client);
    }
    //...
```

All the active connections will be updated every time the server requests the CouchDB list function. Also, the results of that request will be cached:

```
mapchat = {
    //sendChatClusters:function()...

    getChatClusters: function(){
        db.spatiallist("geo/proximity-clustering/recentPoints",
                        {"bbox":"-180,-90,180,90",
                         "sort":"true",
                         "limit":"5",
                         "nopoints":"true"},
                function(er, docs) {
                    if(er){sys.puts("Error: "+sys.inspect(er));return;}
                    mapchat.clusters = docs;
                    mapchat.sendChatClusters();
                    // Check the clustered chat locationed every 10 mins.
                    setTimeout(mapchat.getChatClusters, (1000*600));
                }
            }
        }
    }
}
```

To start the first check of the clustered chat locations simply call the `getChatClusters` function:

```
mapchat.getChatClusters();
```

Every ten minutes the server will check with CouchDB for the curent clustered points and send that to the connected clients. The client will add those points to a list, and add click events to those list items so users can navigate to other active conversations on the map.

Display List of Clusters in the Client

The client needs to handle a new message type, `clusters`:

```
var chat = {
    displayChatClusters: function(clusters){
        $("div#clusters ul").empty();
        for(c in clusters){
            center = [clusters[c].center.coordinates[1],
                        clusters[c].center.coordinates[0]].join(",");
            image_url = "http://maps.google.com/maps/api/staticmap?center=" +
                center + "&zoom=4&size=80x40&sensor=true"
            $li = $("<li><img src='"+image_url+"' />"+
                    "<div class='location'>"+clusters[c].locationName+"</div></li>");
            $("div#clusters ul").append($li);
            $li.data("location", center);
            $li.click(function(e){
                lat =$(this).data("location").split(",")[0];
```

```
        lon = $(this).data("location").split(",")[1];
        map.setCenter(new google.maps.LatLng(lat,lon));
      });
    }
  }
};
```

By adding a bit of styling, images from Google Maps API, and context from SimpleGeo, the clustered points become a well-presented list of recent chat messages, as seen in Figure 4-2.

Figure 4-2. List of Chat Clusters

There is the completed project, MapChat. A demo version of MapChat is hosted at *http://mapchat.im* and the source code is available at *http://github.com/dthompson/map chat*. MapChat makes good use of real-time communications via Node.js. It handles saving and querying geo-tagged chat messages using CouchDB. It also renders those messages on the map for users to interact with, by making use of the Google Maps API. This quick demo shows the power of getting started with geospatial data using Node.js and CouchDB.

About the Author

Mick Thompson has been developing code using open source tools for 10 years. He is passionate about open source, web applications, and API design. He has worked almost exclusively for startups where building applications on new and innovative technologies is the norm. Since location has become more available on mobile devices in the last few years, he has focused his attention at enhancing existing projects with geolocation.

Colophon

The animal on the cover of *Getting Started with GEO, CouchDB, and Node.js* is a fifteen-spined stickleback (*Spinachia spinachia*).

The cover image is from *Johnson's Natural History*. The cover font is Adobe ITC Garamond. The text font is Linotype Birka; the heading font is Adobe Myriad Condensed; and the code font is LucasFont's TheSansMonoCondensed.

Get even more for your money.

Join the O'Reilly Community, and register the O'Reilly books you own. It's free, and you'll get:

- $4.99 ebook upgrade offer
- 40% upgrade offer on O'Reilly print books
- Membership discounts on books and events
- Free lifetime updates to ebooks and videos
- Multiple ebook formats, DRM FREE
- Participation in the O'Reilly community
- Newsletters
- Account management
- 100% Satisfaction Guarantee

Signing up is easy:

1. **Go to: oreilly.com/go/register**
2. **Create an O'Reilly login.**
3. **Provide your address.**
4. **Register your books.**

Note: English-language books only

To order books online:
oreilly.com/store

For questions about products or an order:
orders@oreilly.com

To sign up to get topic-specific email announcements and/or news about upcoming books, conferences, special offers, and new technologies:
elists@oreilly.com

For technical questions about book content:
booktech@oreilly.com

To submit new book proposals to our editors:
proposals@oreilly.com

O'Reilly books are available in multiple DRM-free ebook formats. For more information:
oreilly.com/ebooks

O'REILLY®

Spreading the knowledge of innovators   oreilly.com

The information you need, when and where you need it.

With Safari Books Online, you can:

Access the contents of thousands of technology and business books

- Quickly search over 7000 books and certification guides
- Download whole books or chapters in PDF format, at no extra cost, to print or read on the go
- Copy and paste code
- Save up to 35% on O'Reilly print books
- **New!** Access mobile-friendly books directly from cell phones and mobile devices

Stay up-to-date on emerging topics before the books are published

- Get on-demand access to evolving manuscripts.
- Interact directly with authors of upcoming books

Explore thousands of hours of video on technology and design topics

- Learn from expert video tutorials
- Watch and replay recorded conference sessions

O'REILLY®

Lightning Source UK Ltd.
Milton Keynes UK
UKHW031316190820
368487UK00005B/278